How to Draw Zentangle® Art

DRAWING ZENTANGLE® BUGS AND BUTTERFLIES

Hannah Geddes

Gareth Stevens
PUBLISHING

Acknowledgments

The Zentangle® method was created by Rick Roberts and Maria Thomas.

"Zentangle"®, the Zentangle logo, "Anything is possible one stroke at a time", "Bijou", "Certified Zentangle Teacher" ®, "CZT"®, "Zentangle Apprentice"®, and "Zentomology" are trademarks, service marks, or certification marks of Rick Roberts, Maria Thomas, and/or Zentangle Inc.

PERMISSION TO COPY ARTWORKS: The written instructions, designs, patterns, and projects in this book are intended for the personal use of the reader and may be reproduced for that purpose only. Any other use, especially commercial use, is forbidden under law without the written permission of the copyright holder.

All the tangles in this book are Zentangle® originals created by Rick Roberts and Maria Thomas, apart from: Hollibaugh (page 15) by Molly Hollibaugh.

Please visit our website, www.garethstevens.com.
For a free color catalog of all our high-quality books,
call toll free 1-800-542-2595 or fax 1-877-542-2596.

CATALOGING-IN-PUBLICATION DATA

Names: Geddes, Hannah.
Title: Drawing Zentangle® bugs and butterflies / Hannah Geddes.
Description: New York : Gareth Stevens Publishing, 2018. | Series: How to draw Zentangle® art | Includes index.
Identifiers: ISBN 9781538208403 (pbk.) | ISBN 9781538208434 (library bound) | ISBN 9781538208410 (6 pack)
Subjects: LCSH: Drawing--Technique--Juvenile literature. | Repetitive patterns (Decorative arts)--Juvenile literature. |
    Insects in art--Juvenile literature.
Classification: LCC NC730.G43 2018 | DDC 741.201'9--dc23

Published in 2018 by
Gareth Stevens Publishing
111 East 14th Street, Suite 349
New York, NY 10003

Copyright © 2018 Arcturus Holdings Limited

Step-outs and Zentangle® Inspired Artworks by Hannah Geddes
Text by Catherine Ard
Outline illustrations by Katy Jackson
Designed by Trudi Webb and Emma Randall
Edited by Frances Evans

Printed in China

CPSIA compliance information: Batch CS17GS: For further information contact
Gareth Stevens, New York, New York at 1-800-542-2595.

Contents

Insect Inspiration

Zentangle® is a drawing method created by Rick Roberts and Maria Thomas. It teaches you how to create beautiful pieces of art using simple **patterns** called tangles. Tangling is a really fun, relaxing way to get creative, and it brings out the artist in everyone. You can tangle wherever and whenever the mood takes you!

Many people are put off by creepy-crawlies, but when you look closely, their beautiful shapes and patterns can be inspiring. We are going to use these little wonders to help you create some Zentangle® Inspired Artworks ("ZIAs"). Our insect-inspired tangles will make your creepy-crawly creations really dazzle!

Pens and Pencils

Pencils are good for drawing "strings" (page 18) and for adding shade to your tangles. A 01 (0.25-mm) black pen is good for fine lines. Use a 05 (0.45-mm) or 08 (0.50-mm) pen to fill in bigger areas. You can use paints to brighten up your art, too!

Paper

Tangles are usually drawn on a square 3.5-inch (9 cm) tile made of thin cardboard. You can use any kind of paper, but if you want to make your tangles really special, use good quality art paper. Have some tracing paper on hand so you can trace the images in this book to use as outlines for your Zentangle® Inspired Artworks.

Useful Techniques

There are some special techniques you might come across when you tangle. A "highlight" is a gap or blank space in the lines of your tangles. Highlights can make your tangles look shiny!

An "aura" is a line traced around the inside or outside of a shape. Use auras to add a sense of movement to your art.

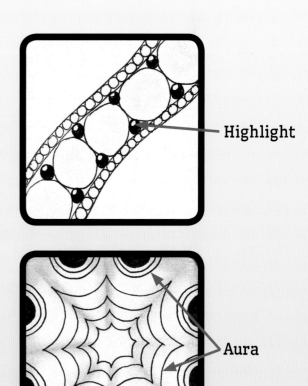

Highlight

Aura

Essential Tangles

Here are some fantastic tangles to get you started! You can practice drawing each tangle on a square tile (see step 1 on page 18 for instructions). Each project in this book has a tangle key that tells you where to find the instructions for the tangles that have been used.

Tipple

1. Start by drawing a small circle on your paper.

2. Add a few more circles around the first one. They can be any size you like.

3. Keep drawing circles of different sizes until the chosen space is full.

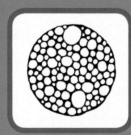

4. Shade in the spaces between the circles to finish your tangle.

Bales

1. Draw evenly-spaced **diagonal** lines across the paper.

2. Draw diagonal lines in the opposite direction to make a **grid**.

3. Draw bumps along the bottom of all of the lines you drew in step 1.

4. Then draw bumps along the top of these lines.

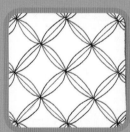

5. Repeat steps 3 and 4 on the diagonal lines that you drew in step 2.

6. Your pretty tangle is finished.

Keeko

1. Draw four **horizontal** lines next to each other. They should be the same length and equally spaced apart.

2. Draw another four lines next to the first set, but this time make the lines **vertical**.

3. Repeat steps 1 and 2 until the row is complete.

4. Underneath each set of four horizontal lines, draw a set of four vertical lines.

5. Draw a set of four horizontal lines underneath each set of vertical lines.

6. Fill the chosen area, and then add some shading to finish it.

Cadent

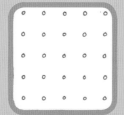    

1. Draw a grid made up of small circles.

2. Draw a curve from the top of the first circle to the bottom of the second circle.

3. Repeat this pattern across each horizontal row of circles.

4. Now, use the same pattern to join up the vertical lines of circles.

5. Your Cadent tangle is complete.

'Nzeppel

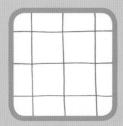 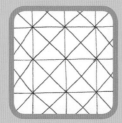 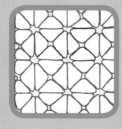

1. Draw horizontal and vertical lines over the paper to make a grid.

2. Now draw diagonal lines in both directions over the paper. They should be evenly spaced so they run through the middle of each square in the grid.

3. Each square in the grid should now be split into four triangular sections. Draw around the shape of each triangle, but round off the corners to create this pebble-like effect.

4. Continue to fill each square with triangles, as shown.

5. Add some shading to finish your tangle.

Printemps

This tangle is perfect for creating swirly **textures**.

1. Draw a dot in the middle of your page. Then begin to draw a small **spiral** starting from the dot.

2. Continue drawing your spiral. You can make it as small or as big as you like.

3. Once the spiral is the size that you want, turn the line in to close up the shape. You should have a smooth circle around the edge.

4. Add more spiral shapes around the first one.

5. Continue drawing Printemps spirals until you have filled the space.

Knightsbridge

This tangle is super easy and eye catching.
Use it to add pizzazz to any picture!

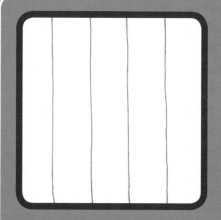

1. Start by drawing evenly-spaced vertical lines across your paper.

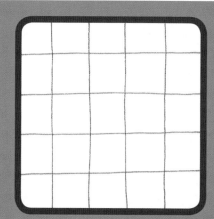

2. Now add the same number of horizontal lines to make a grid.

3. Use a pen to shade in every other square to create a check pattern.

4. Once you've mastered this simple grid pattern, you can customize it however you like.

Tangle Tip!
Change the look of this tangle by using diagonal lines to create your grid!

Fracas

Take a tip from our eight-legged friends and work this wonderful web tangle into your insect pictures.

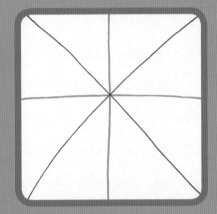

1. Draw two diagonal lines from corner to corner to make an "X" on the paper.

2. Add a vertical and a horizontal line across the middle.

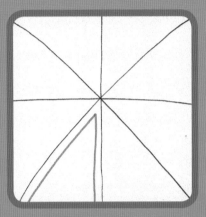

3. Draw lines inside one of the triangle sections as shown, leaving a small gap.

4. Repeat inside each triangle.

5. Now draw thick, evenly-spaced stripes inside each triangle and fill them in.

6. Add some pencil shading along the edges of the triangles and blend to finish.

Emingle

Give your pictures a classic twist with this Greek-inspired spiral tangle.

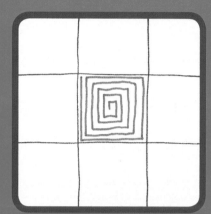

1. Draw evenly-spaced vertical and horizontal lines to create a grid.

2. Starting in the middle of one of the squares, draw a straight-edged spiral to fill the shape.

3. Repeat in each square, drawing the spirals in the same direction each time.

4. Your tangle is complete!

Tangle Tip!
If you shade the middle of each spiral you can give Emingle a **3-D** effect!

W2

Create a really wacky look with this wonderful basket weave tangle!

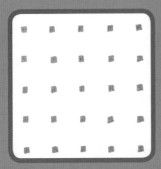

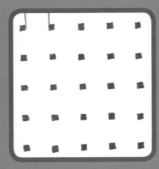

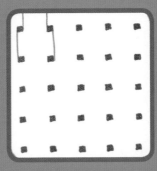

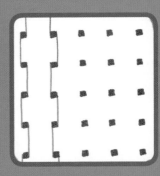

1. Start by drawing rows of small, evenly-spaced squares. Fill in the squares with your pen.

2. Draw a line from the top of the paper to the right edge of the top left square. Now draw a line to the left edge of the next square.

3. Connect these two squares to the squares below. Draw the lines on the outside edges.

4. Repeat steps 2 and 3 until you reach the bottom of the paper, alternating between the inside and outside edges.

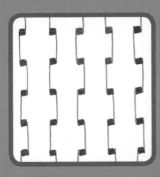

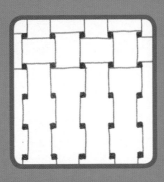

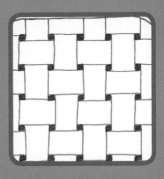

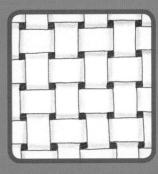

5. Continue working your way down the vertical rows, alternating the lines each time.

6. Now start drawing lines across the horizontal rows, alternating the lines between the top and bottom edges of the squares.

7. Continue adding lines until all of the squares are joined up.

8. Add shading around the edges of the lines to complete the woven effect.

Hurry

Don't rush! Take your time and this tangle of overlapping lines will look awesome on any bug.

 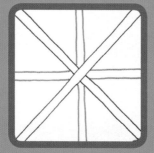 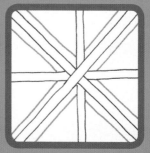 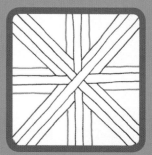

1. Start by drawing a pair of **parallel** lines across the page to make a band. Draw another band in the opposite direction. When you meet the first band, stop drawing and then continue on the other side.

2. Draw a horizontal band and a vertical band across the middle, stopping where you meet another band and continuing on the other side.

3. Draw lines on either side of the diagonal bands, keeping them an even distance apart.

4. Now add lines on either side of the horizontal and vertical bands.

5. Keep adding diagonal, horizontal, and vertical lines in turn.

6. Continue to add lines until you have filled the space.

7. Add shading around the edge of the tangled area.

Hollibaugh

This random tangle makes a great **contrast** to rows of regular patterns.

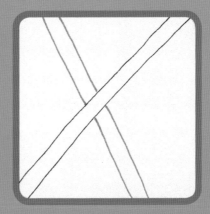

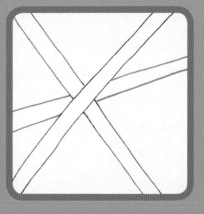

1. Start by drawing a pair of parallel lines across the page to make a band. You can draw the lines in any direction.

2. Draw another band going in a different direction. When you reach the first band, stop drawing and then continue on the other side.

3. Add another band in a different direction than the first two. Stop when you meet any lines and continue on the other side.

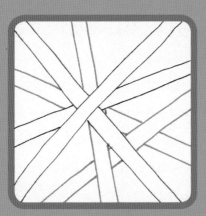

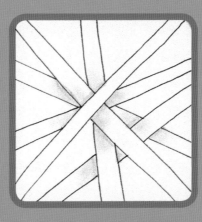

4. Continue to add more bands in different directions until you are happy with the effect.

5. Finally, add shading where each band meets another one.

Tangle Tip!
You could fill the gaps between each band with other tangles, such as Tipple, to add extra detail.

Jetties

Roll out this tangle of marble-like balls whenever a picture needs some striking spots.

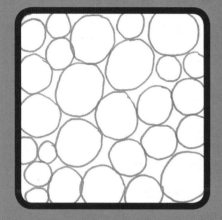

1. Start by drawing a selection of large circles on your paper and then draw some smaller circles in the gaps.

2. On each circle, draw two lines across the middle to form a band and fill them in with your pen. Draw the bands at different angles.

3. Add a line slightly above each band and another line slightly below.

4. Shade with a pencil below each band to finish the tangle off.

Tangle Tip!
Try varying the patterns inside the circles to change the look.

Yincut

This cool, **quilted** tangle is perfect for giving hard objects a soft, padded effect.

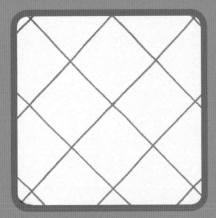

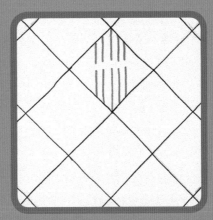

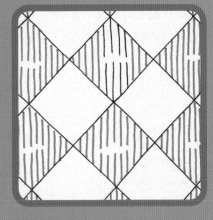

1. Draw evenly-spaced diagonal lines going in both directions across your paper to make a grid of diamonds.

2. In the middle of one of the diamonds, draw 4 or 5 vertical lines, leaving a small gap halfway down.

3. Draw more lines on either side to fill the shape, but this time don't leave a gap. Continue filling the diamonds with lines, leaving every other row of diamonds blank.

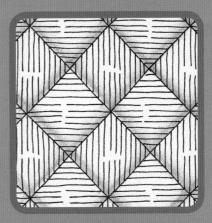

4. Now fill in all the blank diamonds with horizontal lines. Again, leave a little gap in the lines in the middle.

5. Add some pencil shading along the bottom edges of each diamond to complete the tangle.

Strings, Tangles, and ZIAs

The Zentangle® method begins with drawing "strings." These are pencil lines that separate spaces inside a shape. The spaces are then filled with tangles to create your ZIA. Each project in this book starts with an outline of an animal with the strings already drawn in.

These steps show you how to build up a set of Zentangle® patterns on a Zentangle® tile. Tiles are good for practicing the tangles you've just learned. They can also be works of art themselves!

1. To create a square tile, use a ruler and pencil to draw four evenly-spaced dots for the corners. Connect the dots with straight lines.

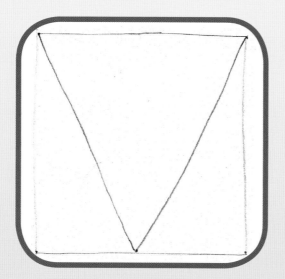

2. Now add strings to divide up the square. Draw a dot in the center of the bottom line. Then draw strings from the top corners to the new dot. This will create three triangle shapes to fill with tangles.

3. Choose a section to fill and a tangle to start with. We've chosen Printemps (page 9). Starting in one corner and using a pen, carefully fill the area with the tangle.

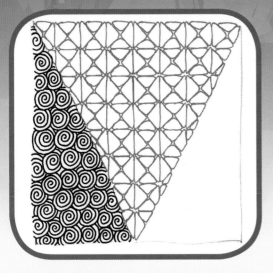

4. Now move to the next space created by the string. We've chosen to fill this section with 'Nzeppel (page 8).

5. In the final space, we've used Bales (page 7).

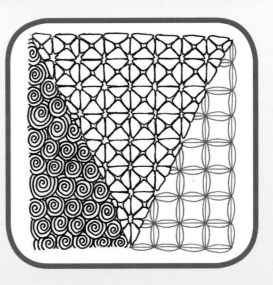

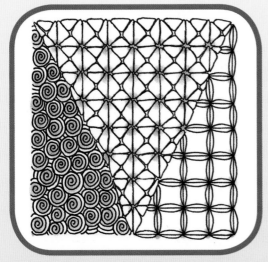

6. To complete the tangles, add shading to create shape and texture.

Now you're ready to start your own tangles!

Spooky Spider

A spider waits patiently for an unsuspecting fly to get tangled in its web. Get tangled up in your own cool, creepy-crawly creation!

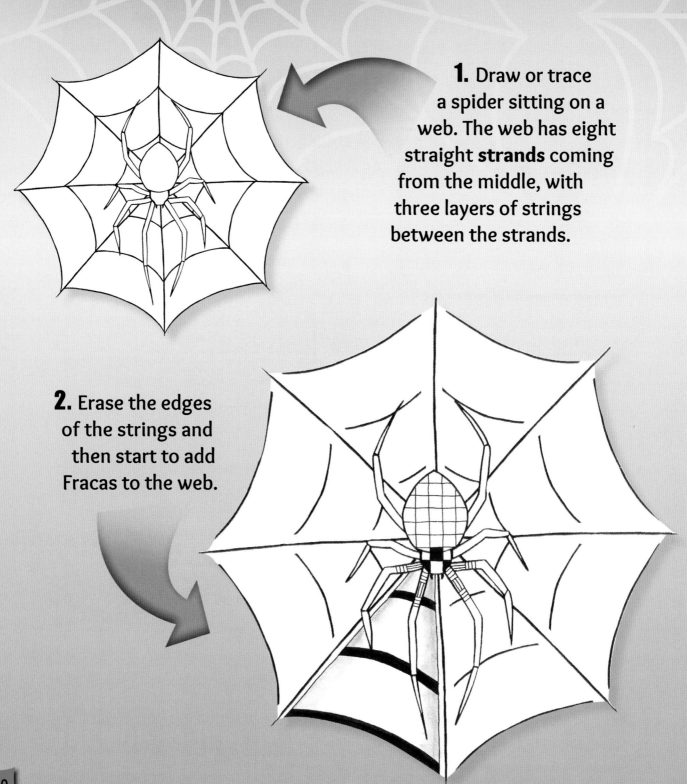

1. Draw or trace a spider sitting on a web. The web has eight straight **strands** coming from the middle, with three layers of strings between the strands.

2. Erase the edges of the strings and then start to add Fracas to the web.

3. We've used Knightsbridge for the body of our spider and Keeko for the legs.

TANGLE KEY
Fracas: page 11
Keeko: page 7
Knightsbridge: page 10

4. Finish off your picture by shading and smudging around the strands of the web.

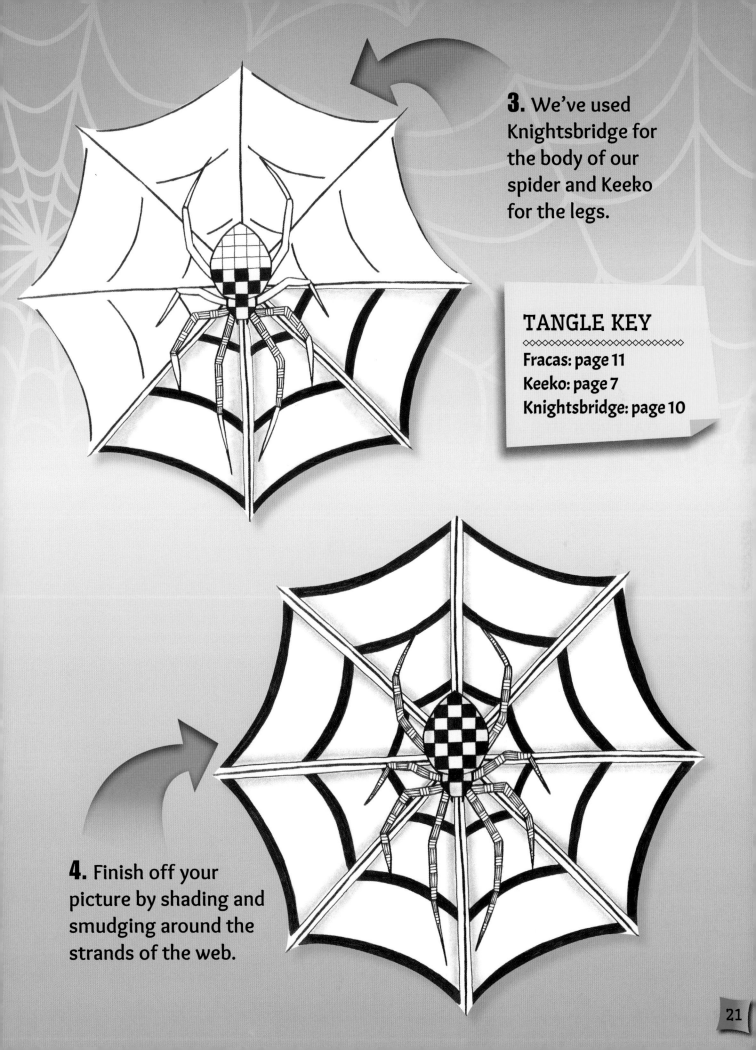

Stag Beetle

The male stag beetle has impressive jaws that look like a deer's **antlers**. Create your own beetle with tangled jaws and open wings, ready to fight or take flight!

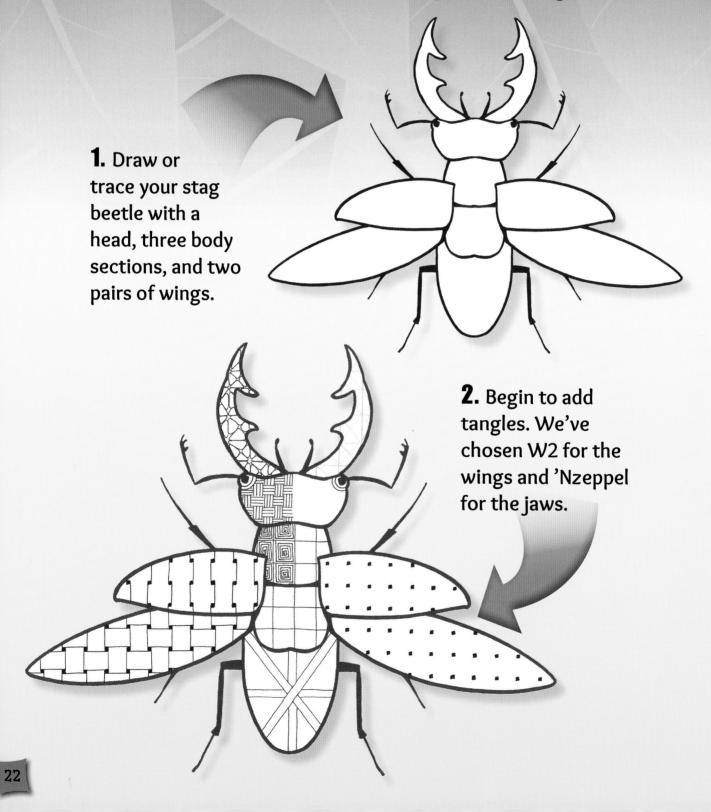

1. Draw or trace your stag beetle with a head, three body sections, and two pairs of wings.

2. Begin to add tangles. We've chosen W2 for the wings and 'Nzeppel for the jaws.

3. We used Emingle for the middle sections of the body and Hurry for the end section. Keeko works well for the head.

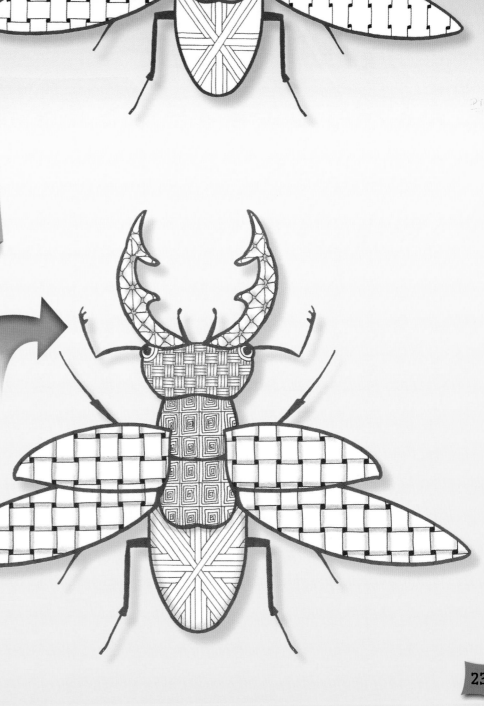

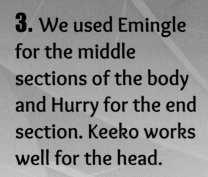

TANGLE KEY

Emingle: page 12
Hurry: page 14
Keeko: page 7
'Nzeppel: page 8
W2: page 13

4. Add some pencil shading to your tangles to complete the picture.

Darting Dragonfly

Dragonflies can **dart** quickly to and fro, up and down, or even stop and **hover**. Follow these steps to create your own fantastic flyer with a matching pair of delicately tangled wings.

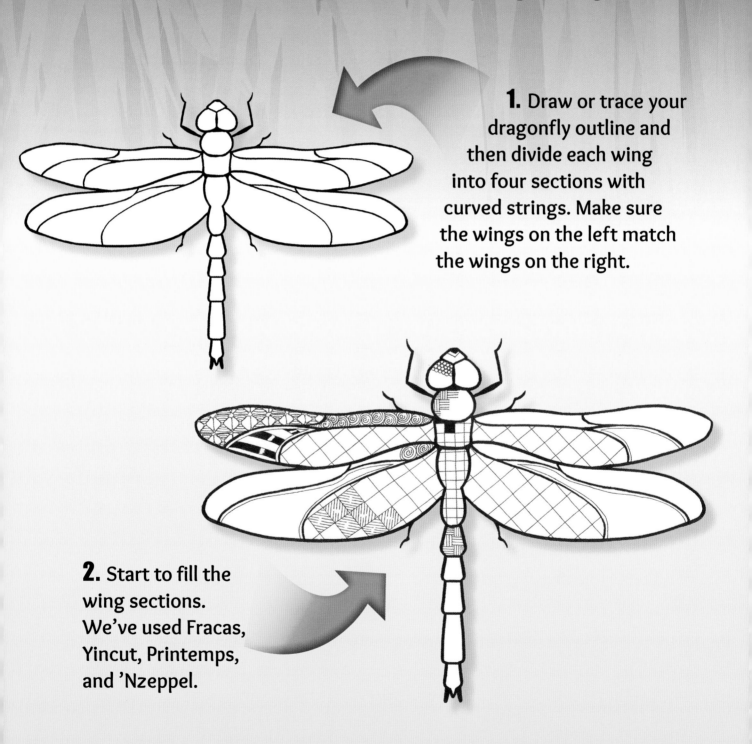

1. Draw or trace your dragonfly outline and then divide each wing into four sections with curved strings. Make sure the wings on the left match the wings on the right.

2. Start to fill the wing sections. We've used Fracas, Yincut, Printemps, and 'Nzeppel.

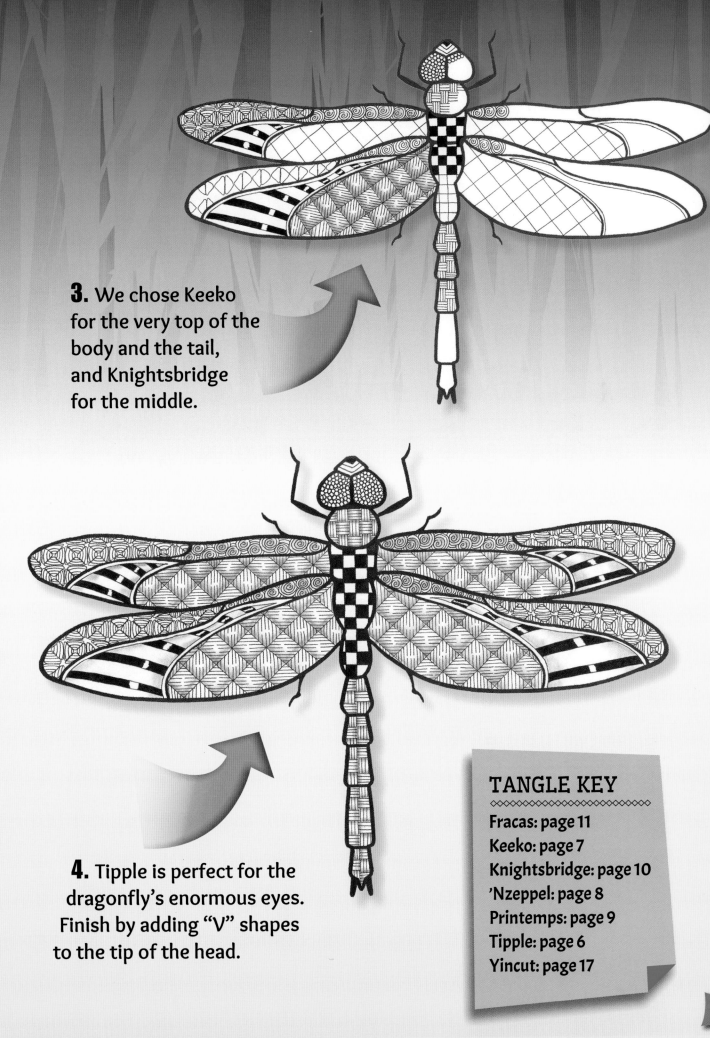

3. We chose Keeko for the very top of the body and the tail, and Knightsbridge for the middle.

4. Tipple is perfect for the dragonfly's enormous eyes. Finish by adding "V" shapes to the tip of the head.

TANGLE KEY

Fracas: page 11
Keeko: page 7
Knightsbridge: page 10
'Nzeppel: page 8
Printemps: page 9
Tipple: page 6
Yincut: page 17

Buzzy Bee

In summer, gardens hum with the sound of bees busily collecting **nectar**. Creating a buzz of your own is easy — just follow the steps to tangle this bold bee!

1. Draw or trace a bee outline. Divide the body into six sections and the wings into three sections.

2. Start to fill the head and body sections with tangles. We've chosen 'Nzeppel, Printemps, Keeko, and Emingle, with W2 in the middle section to create contrast.

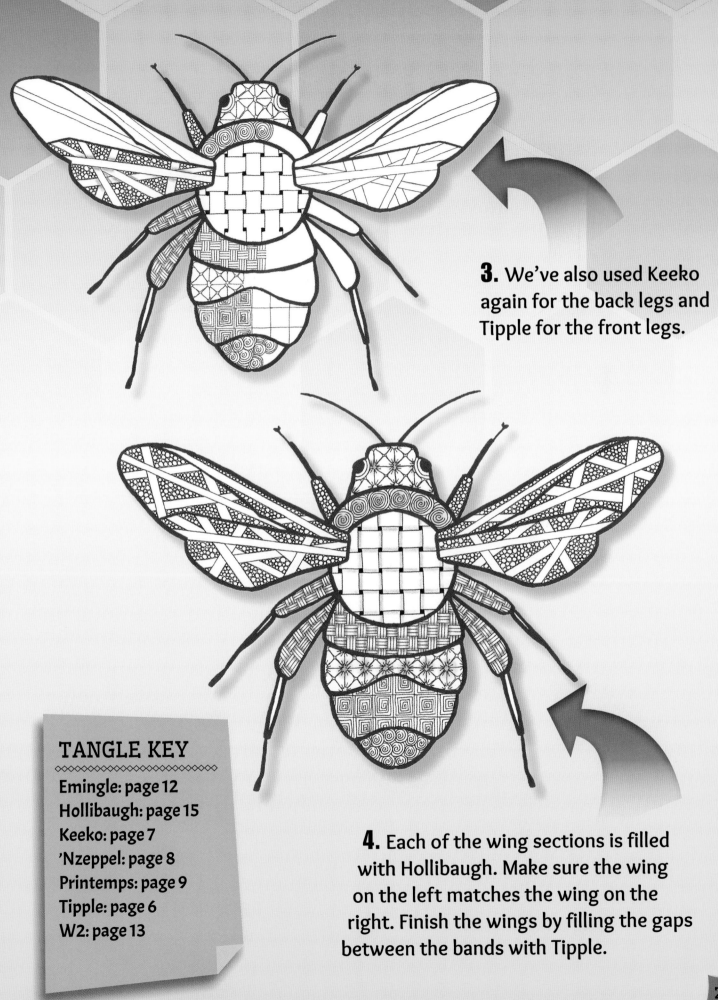

3. We've also used Keeko again for the back legs and Tipple for the front legs.

4. Each of the wing sections is filled with Hollibaugh. Make sure the wing on the left matches the wing on the right. Finish the wings by filling the gaps between the bands with Tipple.

TANGLE KEY

Emingle: page 12
Hollibaugh: page 15
Keeko: page 7
'Nzeppel: page 8
Printemps: page 9
Tipple: page 6
W2: page 13

Beautiful Butterfly

Butterflies are famous for their bright patterns and fluttering flight. Create a pretty butterfly of your own with a pair of beautifully tangled wings.

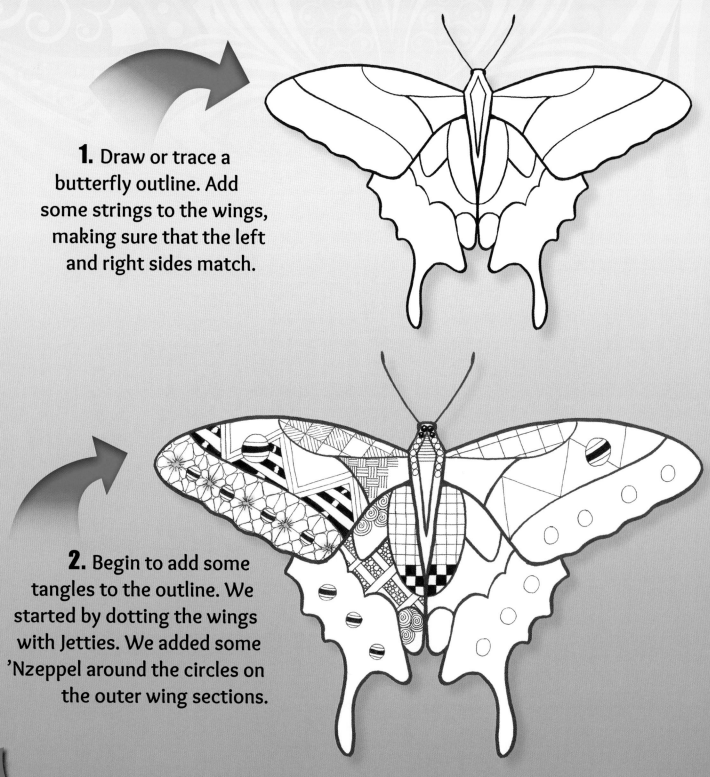

1. Draw or trace a butterfly outline. Add some strings to the wings, making sure that the left and right sides match.

2. Begin to add some tangles to the outline. We started by dotting the wings with Jetties. We added some 'Nzeppel around the circles on the outer wing sections.

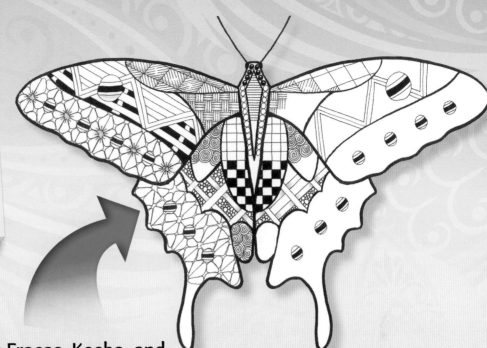

3. We chose Fracas, Keeko, and Yincut for the remaining sections of the upper wings. We've filled the body with some little circles.

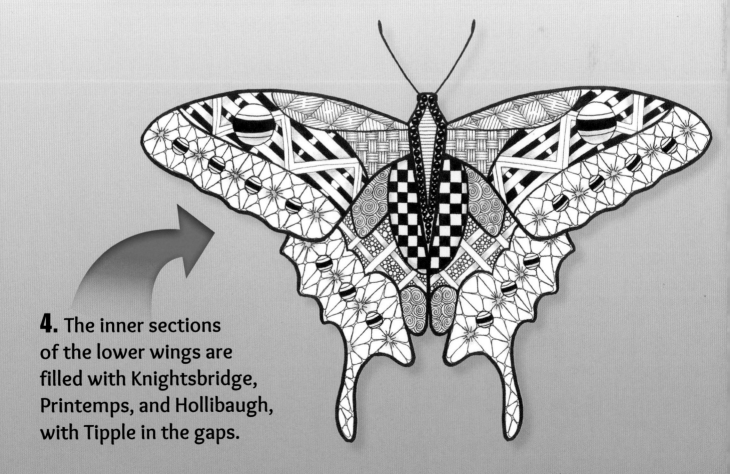

4. The inner sections of the lower wings are filled with Knightsbridge, Printemps, and Hollibaugh, with Tipple in the gaps.

Glossary

3-D Stands for "3-dimensional." If a drawing or pattern looks 3-D, it looks like a solid object.

antler A branched horn that grows from the top of a male deer's head.

contrast To be strikingly different from something else.

dart To move quickly and suddenly.

diagonal A straight line at an angle.

grid A set of uniform squares made from straight lines or points.

horizontal A straight line that is parallel to the horizon, the imaginary line where the ground meets the sky.

hover To stay in one place in the air.

nectar A sweet substance produced by flowers, to encourage bees and other insects to feed from them.

parallel Two lines that run in the same direction at an equal distance apart.

pattern A set of shapes or a design that is repeated.

quilted Layers of fabric sewn together with a diagonal pattern.

spiral A shape made from a line moving outwards in a circular pattern from a central point.

strand A length of fine, string-like fiber.

texture The look or feel of a surface.

vertical A line or object that stands straight up, at right angles with the horizon.

Further Information

Books to Read

How to Draw Butterflies and Other Insects
Peter Gray
PowerKids Press, 2014

Zentangle® for Kids
Jane Marbaix
Sterling Children's Books, 2015

Zentangle® for Kids: With Tangles, Templates, and Pages to Tangle On
Beate Winkler
Quarry Books, 2016

Websites

Visit this website for lots of butterfly and bug coloring pages!
http://www.supercoloring.com/coloring-pages/insects

Head over to this website for lots of Zentangle® coloring pages and other drawing tutorials.
http://www.supercoloring.com/coloring-pages/arts-culture/zentangle

Check out this website for Zentangle® coloring pages and lots of other activity ideas.
http://kidsactivitiesblog.com/?s=zentangle

Publisher's note to educators and parents: Our editors have carefully reviewed these websites to ensure that they are suitable for students. Many websites change frequently, however, and we cannot guarantee that a site's future contents will continue to meet our high standards of quality and educational value. Be advised that students should be closely supervised whenever they access the Internet.

Index